Bebakhshid

Bebakhshid

Nina Mosall

ARP Books | Winnipeg

ARP Books (Arbeiter Ring Publishing)
205-70 Arthur Street
Winnipeg, Manitoba
Treaty 1 Territory and Historic Métis Nation Homeland
Canada R3B 1G7
arpbooks.org

Cover design and interior layout by Relish New Brand Experience.
Printed and bound in Canada by Imprimerie Gauvin on certified FSC ® paper.

ARP Books acknowledges the generous support of the Manitoba
Arts Council and the Canada Council for the Arts for our publishing
program. We acknowledge the financial support of the Government of
Canada and the Province of Manitoba through the Book Publishing
Tax Credit and the Book Publisher Marketing Assistance Program of
Manitoba Culture, Heritage, and Tourism.

Library and Archives Canada Cataloguing in Publication

Title: Bebakhshid / Nina Mosall.
Names: Mosall, Nina, author.
Description: Poems.
Identifiers: Canadiana (print) 20230224504 | Canadiana (ebook)
    20230224520 | ISBN 9781927886748 (softcover) | ISBN 9781927886755
    (ebook)
Classification: LCC PS8626.08155 B43 2023 | DDC C811/.6—dc23

For maman and baba.

Contents

My Most Pleasant Morning

"Assalamu alaikum"
 Greeting from the morning
 Mother brushes my hair
 dark and frizzy
 difficult to manage
 She pushes the wooden brush
 from top
 to bottom
 We eat walnuts and cheese
 dark tea
 with milk for me
 sour cherry jam
 my father loves to place
 on bread
 generously
 He tells me about riding
 his first motorcycle
 curly hair flowing
 I wish I could have seen it
 He lost his photos
 but god whispers
"good morning" anyways

Ash and Yogurt

I say my prayers
loudly
before we lift off

Mikham beram khooneh

A man in a hound's-tooth jacket
(whose eyes are two lakes,
whose skin has a touch of snow)
watches
curious to see
me. Hijabi.
I pray for my mother
who watches
a 20 hour flight
She is watching
from her window
for a plane
A plane
to recite:
Another daughter has left
Another daughter
who drinks black tea with her in the morning
watching the street vendors set up shop
listening to her gossip
of middle-aged friends

Another daughter
who helps stir the pot of ash
always requesting more yogurt
to lighten dark bowls of green

Kei bar migardi?
When will you come home?
Mikham beram khooneh
I want to go home
She is watching me in another plane
or maybe my plane
but I cannot see her
Through this oval telescope
her hands (a look of tree bark) do not stroke my hair
her eyes (whirlpools of gold dirt) do not watch me
breathe sharp

We do not bow our heads together and whisper prayers
the hound's-tooth man cannot understand
Delam barat tang shode
I miss you

Cinquains

Iranian New Years

Gold coins
line the table
A red apple, a date
Sister slips me two kolouches
A smile

My father

He sits
on the green couch
Listens to Prince, smokes slow
Tells me about time in Shiraz
Day dreams

We Have Our Ups and Downs, Too

1
We sit in circles
eat saffron rice, kebab, tea
Hear the rain knocking

2
He comes over once
takes shoes off by the carpet
Mother smiles (he's in!)

3
When you wake up from
a nap, eat fresh fruit. That's what
Mother, Father says

4
A week since brother
Yusef came back. Night shifts
left his eyes wide open

5
She liked you too much
Halo your head in esfand
Once, twice, three times. Again

Our Haikus

1

"Go back home"
But home is chai and Mother
both two blocks away

2

I don't show you my
legs today. Hair outlines me
I don't grow like others

3

Should I laugh? You call
me aggressive. It's the news
that gets to you, friend

4

Pray for a safe flight
We kneel by the gates, hands open
Flight attendants glare

They Can Call You Whatever They Want

They call you
foreign
to Canada
to the language
that trips your tongue-
makes you repeat
To the french fries
you used to cook for them
Couldn't find a job
that didn't want you
for the minimum

They call you
Muslim
because you have brown eyes
black eyebrows
that weigh you down
make you look serious
make them think
you have a
problem

Radical
must be your thoughts

They don't know
that you're Muslim,
that you pray for a safe life
for your family.
That it helps you fight the demons
at night
when *nazar* isn't good enough
When your past floods in
through the ceiling
the news
they call you
other names
Other

And I can't bear to hear them
you won't let me
hear them
Loud mouths
closed fists
Frowns that overshadow
my portrait of you
hanging by the front door
Father

Down With Luck

My mother has told me
she has no way to pay for
school
I raise my head and say
"I'll find the money."

At work I'm paid
minimum wage
Clean toilet bowls
eat leftover caviar
the gentleman and woman leave
beside an eighty dollar tip
(For the server, of course)
I raise my head
At least I have something
to warm my insides

At three a.m., I walk home
I need to stay awake
finish my paper
on Independence Day
I feel warm liquid
on the back of my neck
"Dirty A-rab"
I don't look behind me
I raise my head
towards the direction of home

Payman Prays

Payman tries to find God, but it's hard to see in the dark
When the other students mock the accent
Cuts him deep, leaves a mark

At night he writes in his journal
the one Mother gave before he left her sunflower garden, her
      honey sweets
Payman tries to find God, but it's hard to see in the dark

"You can call me Peter if it's easier."
He smiles, shakes the hand of the 7/11 manager
Cuts him deep, leaves a mark

You can't have a hot plate, a refrigerator, a toaster oven here
He remembers his father's tahdig, the flakiness of crisp rice
Payman tries to find God, but it's hard to see in the dark

Pastor Daniel invites him over for dinner
The family wears cashmere sweaters. White teeth. Eyes that
      glisten in candlelight
Cuts him deep, leaves a mark

Payman surrounds himself with photos. Mother picking a
      white daisy. Brother winking
They paint themselves in his mind
Payman tries to find God, but it's hard to see in the dark
Cuts him deep, leaves a mark

Am i racist? BAD EXPERIENCES WITH MIDDLE EASTERN PEOPLE

Found poem from yahoo answers

hi,
i think i might be.
Arabs, muzlims, afghanis-
a few experiences
that were bad.

i didn't use to feel
this way.
But now…

in my college classes
we talk
about the middle east,
how bad iran is!
It's causing me to become.

It wasn't my fault
the computer wasn't working.
The middle eastern man wanted to talk
to my supervisor but
it wasn't my fault.

Not to mention
the whole war that's happening-
I know it's bad,
but I can't help it.
But now I'm starting to become.
any advice?

We Journey To Judgement

1
They shouldn't enter
Haven't they taken enough?
Canada needs less

2
It took me two boat
Rides to get here and you say
I should turn around?

3
Mother tried to help
But when water comes over
We tend to migrate

4
Nasar was nine months
I could hold her feet in one palm
but she slipped through me

Small losses matter
It slips through you
like Nasar, lost at sea

5
I miss dinner time
sitting on the floor with tea
Weight of work takes you

6
Welcome to your home
They lie to our faces—
haven't seen them since

7
The women wrap their
heads in cotton, delicate
designs you call "attack."

8
My father reads in
Farsi—Hafez, Rumi. An
escape from the West

A Woman of Iran

Inspired by Shirin Nashat's "Rebellious Silence"

I am repression in this country
but my country is not
a cemented ground,
grey and uniformed
It is a flowing
yellow floral hijab
that frames my face
my faith

I am freedom—
my hair mine
to comb
and present in the soft lights
of my bedroom
of my lover's eyes
I tempt

How dare I hold my partner's hand
picking pomegranates and
sunflower seeds seasoned in lime
in the busy market
in crowds of men
I am to blame
fifty lashings or one hundred cash
I cannot earn respect either way

Iran Had Grunge, Too

"Iran had grunge, too."
She turns up the volume

We are nestled
between three cars and a wall
This parking lot
had a small accident
"You'll probably have to wait
an hour."
He wore fluorescent yellow
carried a flashlight
though you could see the bright
grey sky
From the entrance of the parking lot

My mother shows me Iranian grunge
in her light blue PT Cruiser
Pluckings of an electric guitar
a droning "la lala,"
a sad voice
I imagine my father in his teens
long hair and cigarettes
behind his ears
His voice looks like him

I google his face:
Dark, wide eyed
he's smoked a lot of joints
I can tell
"He's still alive
they used to always
say he died."
How strange is it
to live
while you've been mourned
in people's eyes

I turn the volume up
we drone on

Immigrant Haikus

"I told you in small pieces"

1
When will we get paid?
Sing to my mom "it'll come soon,"
but I cannot lie

2
When the towers fell
I could not understand them
Am I terror?

3
My father drove taxi
Downtown isn't pretty at night
when people point guns

4
They saved up for years
We never had new school clothes:
outgrew our roots

"I wanted you to reach it"

1
Her skin rosewater
Warm like the heater back home
far away, too

2
Smoke obstructed dreams
my lungs filled with ash, I scream
cough up foreign guilt

3
He chased me. Yellow
is all I saw. 5 minutes
to know my worth. Ok

4
Our nails are purple
Tearing up, she sends prayer:
"wrap us up in red"

How r u

You write to me
 small poems
Text messages
 badly written

"Lazania's in the fridge"

You can't spell
A sorry story
 of your hard work

"20 dollars
 under yur door."

So I can buy that book
 on baking cupcakes
 I raved about for so long

"I love u xxx"

Three x's
 to make me feel
 what you felt
 the moment
 I became a part

of your body
You've hand picked
these words
Spelt them aloud
spoken
aloud
to make sure there's no mistake
to make sure
I know

I only check messages occasionally
Sometimes wish
I'd make a phone call
instead

"Gudnite my luv."

Esfand

"She gave you the evil eye." You smile at Mother and look around the kitchen. White tiles. A spot of red. Probably crushed tomato from the spaghetti you made. "It's so dry." "It's Iranian." The woman left the room before Mother could cast her out. Quran. Grandmother's blood red beads. We pray under our breaths. "You're so beautiful. I wish I had a daughter. I wish I had a daughter as beautiful as you." Fabricated. Her hair is too long for you to trust her. "I won't let you deal with this." Mother takes out *esfand*. Seeds. You remember the name because it smells so bad. Like black burning rubber. Your dad always hated having to replace tires. He wants to drive on Highway 15 uninterrupted. You can hear crackles. Mother has the stove on high heat. Aluminum cradles the reeking seeds. Burning. You can smell the rubber and your eyes water. Jordan told you your food looked like green goo. But you loved your Mother's stew. You look at the guest room door. Exit. Mother hovers the *esfand* over you like a halo, rotating it clockwise, counterclockwise, clockwise. Islamic Angel. She re-traces your steps into the kitchen, stretching the bad smell out like chewing gum. You follow where God leads. "*Cheshmeh shoor,*" Mother mutters. Evil eye.

The Beginning of Dawn

We waver to the mosque
Mother wraps my head in cotton
lace
and a kiss
Fajr is in the air
seeping through us
a whispering *imam*
We miss the garden

In the early morning
the sun rises
we fall to our knees
There are no bruises
Pillows kiss our cartilage
cradle our base
so we can sing service
sweet

If you see our palms touch
our temples
think of Mother's garden:
mint grows out of corners
We smash them
into the bottoms of our cups
I grow here
There are no ceilings

here
I see a well full of honey
the liquid lags behind
cloaking us in
syrup and *salahs*

This is a Jihad

Mother cooks *berenj*
every other evening
The rice shines golden
from saffron and butter
We tried to make the same
boiling grains, measuring salt-
viscous bowls of rice
we pretend is as good

At night she drops to her knees
bows her head, and prays
for us. We haven't learned to pray yet
peek from behind the beige walls
want to hear her whisper
"Hayya 'alas salah,
Hayya 'alas salah."
This is a jihad
for us. Our backs ache
after seconds of bowing
our knees grow numb
and we forget the words
to Allah's heart

At night
Mother gently brushes our thick
coarse hair
She helps us dress in gowns
lays us within an expanse
of pillows and blankets
and reads the *Quran*

"May Allah cause his face to shine,
the man who hears what I say
and conveys it to others."
She leaves a scent
of saffron, with questions of a *mujahid*
We squeeze our pillows close
hoping the moon shines on our beds

Who Hears Hasan

It hasn't even been a week
since he left the holy book
at the end of a park bench
taking a blunt and
sunflower seeds with him
He fingers *tasbih* daily
The prayer beads' green patterns
fade with each
rub
Allahu Akbar
Allahu Akbar
Allahu Akbar

He sprinkles seeds on the sidewalk
tries to grow
to spell
man komak kon—
guide me
guide me
guide me

It hasn't even been a week
before he decides prayer
isn't his thing anymore
He wants to yell

cross his arms
furrow his black brows
Answer me
answer me
answer me

Today
when he turns corners
esfand rushes to the nostrils—
the wild rue smells like
burnt leaves
Smoke rises from him

He talks to God
through blurred visions
on his front steps
the door to his bedroom
the distant call
of his mother
Hasan, are you there?
I thought I heard you
come in.

They Make Us Have the Same Story

1
Your dad works at a convenience store
selling rainbow slurpees and lotto tickets
behind scratched protective plastic

Your dad works as a taxi driver
weaves through heavy traffic
holds his breath when they hand him cash
and ask for change

2
In high school they called you "Sandy"
even though your name is Donya
They get distracted by olive skin
in white hallways

3
There's nothing sweet about
being a Brownie
it leaves a bitter trace
along your throat
like the words they hurled
inside you, to
rest
at the bottom of your stomach
and rot

4
Your friend called you a terrorist
when your black brows met in the middle
agitated about your stolen bank card
Don't blow the place up
she said, trying to hold in laughter

It Watches You Through the Dashboard

The evil eye hangs
above the front door
My bedroom has three of them
above my bed
my door
and one above my closet

Father wants me to focus on myself
I've never thought
of letting him down, especially
after seeing lines forming
around his Adam's apple
He always taps the evil eyes in my home
just in case
his luck has run out

I remember
the gold plated symbol of Allah
hanging on the dashboard
when he used to drive yellow cars
He used to tell me to
count my blessings
when turning into the depot
"At one point
you'll notice them getting smaller."
He counts circles on the eyes, now

The amount of circles on the evil eye
is the amount of times we've had
health scares
His shakiness makes me
want to hold him still
with prayers
The red and blue carpet carries us
comforts our knees and
his old age
his shaky knees and hands
the stumbling and stuttering through
Zuhr

I memorize
Read thoroughly and with intent
make sure my chants are certain
just to settle his nerves
During the holidays
I receive another evil eye
this one larger and heavier than I have ever
confronted
I decide not to hang it
hide it in a drawer
under blue socks and yellow toques
He doesn't need to count anymore

I Dream of Your Flowers

Even though you didn't ask
I set your chair at the breakfast table
placing brown and white sugar cubes beside it
I know you'll only bite half
of one
leave the rest for flies

Even though you didn't ask
I open the passenger door
lead you out with one hand
Our fingers
point home

Even though you didn't ask
I tell you that "things can change, *inshallah*,"
but you haven't spoken to your sister
in eleven years
I'd rather see you smile half-heartedly
the crinkling around your eyes grow deeper each year

Even though you didn't ask
I call you every evening
It's not hard
to tell you're sitting on the couch
snacking on dill flavoured sunflower seeds
putting your feet up

letting my mundane stories
wash over you like the first spring
bath you had as a child in Tehran
Flower petals rained over you
by women in your neighborhood
I would have never known

Even though you didn't ask
I need to tell you—
sometimes I have trouble sleeping
I dream of intruders and demons
seeping under my front door
flooding me
I want you to know
I'm afraid of drowning
without knowing why there were flowers
in your first bath
Even though you didn't ask
I need you to pull me out
I need you to let me ask

International Star Registry

You would take your time
laying the pink blanket
on grass
We'd spread out tea,
bread, feta cheese, and that cherry syrup
you stole from Mother's stash

"I always wanted a star
named after me"
Pushing your large spectacles
back
mouth wrinkling a smile at me
You sigh

You who flew undocumented
a refugee of many sorts
Of country, community
and self
Who slipped a twenty
in documents, saying
"I can't go home,
I won't go home."
An insistence I wish I had
Who worked three jobs
in one evening
while Mother waited in Turkey

sleeping against the front door
knife in hand
Who held my fresh pinkie finger
in the hospital
"I've never seen someone this
small
    occupy my life so largely."

A patient father, who tells me
"wait a few more minutes:
    the tea will be
    perfect then."
    In this night
    of cheese, bread, and cherry syrup
    Star

I Wish It Would Rain Again

When the rain stops, my mother decides to garden for the
first time in ten years. The front lawn is bare. Overcast.
Beside the patches of yellowing grass, nothing is alive. Five
cars in the driveway. Most of them are Toyotas. She takes
a shovel from the shed. Packets of seeds she got for free
at Safeway. A male cashier she trusted. He looked down
slightly when talking to her. A brother. She walks towards
the front lawn. Nobody's home but she and I. She sprouts
gloves from her pocket. A hose from her stomach. A hat
from her head.

I forget she is my mother in her straw hat. She must have
bought it cheap at the flea market. A Sunday I'd never
remember. Maybe I wandered off. Maybe I had never come
along. They sold potted plants at the entrance. Five dollars
for three daisy pots. A grey curtain of sky is opening up.
Light from the crack spotlights my mother. She is small.
Slightly limping. Reminds me of a jagged tree branch.
I sit on the steps of our front door. The light follows
her. The light slightly touches the ends of her worn out
shoes, as if she is a holy figure, a guide to a greater place.
Empty dirt plots.

She turns to face me. Maybe this time it'll work, she says. I'm unsure if she's speaking to me. Grey skies and a yellow straw hat bend down towards the grass. My mother has planted herself. She straightens her back and digs her roots into the ground. It starts to rain.

It'll work. You'll see, it'll work, I say. Spotlight fades. I'm unsure for the second time today.

I Don't Have Many Memories

She keeps hard caramel candies in her bag
even though she can't have any
"You've got diabetes.
No more fried chicken and sweets for you,
Ms. Mahdavi."

Trying to clean the place up
she takes the wooden broom
and swings blindly at ceiling lights
"It's spotless," I say
When she's fast asleep
I clean the grey cobwebs and dead flies
in the dark living room

Once she told me that the ocean
would swallow me whole
We sat on the bench in front of waves
crashing into logs
a running dog
Her grandchild drowned in a river
thirty-three years ago

Long distance phone calls never made me feel
the distance
"We'll see each other soon,"
she said

It's been so many years
can't remember, seven or eight
I'd still have to travel
to see her in her grave

Small Things

I wish you had it all figured out
when you decided to say yes
Placed that shining rock on your finger
had the baby, the indescribable delight

I wish you figured it out
before he laid a hand on you
the scar on his left cheek
still wakes me up
choking
as if I had one last breath
before I was gone

Two holes in your wall
one in your bedroom door
Your new apartment
broken into
the floor still has broken glass
from the day he didn't want
to go to work

He never did like us

Your own mother wasn't respected by him
She spent half an hour making a turkey sandwich
the way he liked

Eating half
he grunted
threw it in the trash

Shrink

I saw you through the cracked door
dim light
dusty air
Three months since you made your be
the edge of the mattress
a retreat
You committed to sadness
(a disease you couldn't leave)
when he left you
in a dismal bedroom
asylum

I held your hand
you retracted like a knife
The one you were given
as a child
young and exposed
to dirty streets and
dirty minds

Wound open
infected
by dirt stained hands
He left you
and a cracked door

He Couldn't Find His Car Keys

My father is sitting on the front lawn
arms wrapped around his knees

Face unshaven
a vacant lot
Unclear whether or not
to be developed

I take a step from the front door
supposedly leading to another
towards his wilting frame

Instead
the morning dew
cradles my father's knees
tells him he isn't alone

You Had Breakfast with Me Every Tuesday

As if
I didn't miss you
opening
my door
in the stretching time
of morning
nudging me awake
A timid touch
faint whisper
"wake up."
Warm honey

Weight
on the edge of the bed
your presence
in the morning light
Yellow tones
from my window

Breakfast
isn't the same
The smell of toast
golden and inviting
I push away

As if
I didn't miss you
as if you thought I couldn't tell

Short Talk of Eggplants

My mother loves eggplant stew. I am allergic to eggplant. It isn't right. The fruit that reminds her of her purple carpets in Iran. The stew that she shared with her brothers and sisters during school nights when she had been a few years younger than I. Whenever I accidentally eat eggplant, I end up wheezing and rubbing my eyes with fervor. The restaurant menu. I see the eggplant and order it. Sometimes a mistake, honest to god. But sometimes it isn't. At home, I smell the fried eggplants my mother has mastered and my family have grown to love (that I have grown to avoid). I want eggplants to like me. I want to my body to accept what my mother has been preparing since I learned how to breathe.

A Haibun for My Father

As a kid I would take the bus my dad drove. We'd drive to the beach with ruddy gold sand, and then to the depot. The beach, the depot, the beach, the depot, the beach, and then we'd lunch. His break was an hour long. Precisely one hour. Sometimes we'd have fish and chips, and sometimes we'd pack peanut butter and banana or tuna fish sandwiches. I didn't like it when we had fish and chips because we'd have to talk to the host, the waiter, and listen to polka music and the clatter of our cutleries. When we packed our lunches we could sit on the dock and feel the sea breeze. A blanket of salt. Sometimes we would talk, but mainly we would eat our sandwiches and stare at the seagulls. They stood so still I thought they were frozen in time. I can still taste the saltwater when I put my hand in the cold blue flesh.

> Black rubber on waves
> we take the bridge to see birds
> stand like monuments

He Is My Father

We never spoke, and yet we had so much to say
My younger years spent without the worries of the clock
He is my father—the man that tried to talk

At times he recalled moments from his life-mystery
She rejected him because he had a mental block
We never spoke, and yet we had so much to say

Washing my black hair, he tried to teach me history
Mapped out where he failed to escape—tried to walk
He is my father—the man that tried to talk

Coming home from school, he wanted to be sappy
Pat my shoulder, rub my curly head, let words unlock
We never spoke, and yet we had so much to say

He never learned the language, left school and tall buildings early
"They said we'd have a better life here. It's all a crock."
He is my father—the man that tried to talk

For years I wanted to tell him he was okay
He always stuck around, sealed me like caulk
We never spoke and yet we had so much to say
He is my father—the man that tried to talk

It Spans Days

For 5 weeks
I've spent mornings gasping
for air
startled by my own
awakening

In the afternoons
the dishes are
unwashed
the couch
settled in

Watch episodes of some soap
my mother watched when I was young
when I coloured within the lines
biting my tongue
on the living room floor

In the evening
I can't remember what you said
or what I said
but I know how I felt
and how I can't breathe now
and how all I remember
is the broadness of your shoulders
the freckle on the tip of your nose

the way the sky looked
when we met up
by the community center
it was a dark, dark navy sky
we could see all the stars
and you told me you weren't
sure
about us

I remember now
I remember every night
It comes to me like a
cold splash of water
I'd take in the morning
But I'm trying to rest now
and your iced words don't help me sleep

It's In Everything We Don't Say

We sit
on your mother's couch
watching re-runs of
Home Improvement
sipping creamy tea
I want to ask you
about us

The wind outside
whips rain back and forth
hitting windows
the roof
the porch table
We can't hear a thing
under it
Turn up the volume
turn back to where
they're trying to break walls
for a new living room
You avoid eye contact with me
for eight minutes

"How's the tea?"
"I think it'd be great with some
 honey" you say

The wind quiets down
I place my floral cup
on the table
grab a hold of your free hand
squeeze it so tight
I can't tell where my grip
begins and yours ends
We watch them attach
doors, place glass on the windows
rebuild walls

You're in a Crowd

What I couldn't make out:
your eyes
pink lips
soft rounded nose
with a beauty mark on the tip
you called "dirt."
A face I had grown
accustomed to
You'd wait at bus stops:
Newton Exchange
Central Exchange
At the Guildford Exchange
you surprised me with a fruit plate
after class
We sat on round marble
at the park by the mall
eating watermelon and limp grapes
shivering from leftover frost

I didn't recognize you
when I stepped off the bus
Couldn't pick you out
from the cluster
of black backpacks and
oversized hoodies

But when you held me
squeezing tighter
as you reached for fruit
I recognized you

You've Let Me Get Carried Away

You tried to fix the curtains
when I mentioned the sun
creeping through

blinding me from reading
musical history

"How's that?" you ask

I delve into the tunnels
of Vivaldi, Bach
how we still emulate
borrowing patterns,
progressions and tunes
how we still try
to reach their sights
of nature and states of being
fighting one another
You meant the curtains
of course

I Wish There Was An Indent On The Bed

It is morning
I look to my left
A window of mine
I had forgotten
Dusty ledge, a grimy film
covers me
blurring my view
of the frosted outdoors

It is morning
I look to my right
No one is beside me
The bed in disarray
warm
I could stay here all month
cocooned
rolled up so many times
I'd fall inside
disappear

It is morning
In front of me is
a mirror and four cups
each one with drinks
that keep me sober
Coffee, tea

water that tastes like copper
I don't mind
It keeps me awake
at night
so I can stare
blank walls
a blank body
blank face
I don't see much
anymore
but I have time to try

It is morning
You haven't called
I didn't see you leave
and sometimes I wonder
if you ever came
But there is a soft spot
next to me
warm and sunken in
It could have been you
who held me at night
kissing the cold away from my shoulders
blowing hot air
over
and over
Or maybe I rolled over

Top Of The Hill

To have a summer is
to hear some long song
that echoes off lakes
illuminates old campsites

Your cracked lips
my unwashed hair
We smell just fine
Burnt grass and
flat root beer
We feel just fine

I couldn't recall what you said
Something about
aliens and thick clouds
so our feet touch
our eyes sponge the sky
fascination with the stars
masking our embarrassment

It isn't a movie
and we head home
feeling the cold slap of wind
the heat of the sun following
us reliving
marks on the hill

We Took A Ride

Surprised
when I told you
I couldn't ride a bike
you dragged me
to the middle of Kilney's Park

The white sky
blinded your wide eyes
coaxing me
to the top of the hill
"It's beautiful up there,"
"I swear I saw purple sky."

Handlebars
clenched until my knuckles paled
You restrained from telling me
what you meant to say
all along
I understood
the meaning of a push

A Month Earlier

Burnt wood
attached to your sweater
when I told you how I felt
"I think I like you."
The smell stuck to me
after I left

Embarrassed
I avoided you for weeks
"I've got plans,"
"It's getting late."
Excuses I used
the next time we met
at the fire hydrant
burning red in a sticky afternoon
eight blocks from your house

It wasn't long
until your lips curved
a smile
in the still life of the sidewalk
Cherry red
staining your white skin
without an explanation

But you held my hand
the crescent scar
beside your thumb
grazing my own mark
the scene a postcard

Favourite Colour

Your mom thought orange
was an ugly colour
Dress shirts
sneakers and a toque
I could never take my eyes
off the obnoxious glow

A goofy grin
You shared obscure music
the kind with beats made
by a dumpster lid
while locking the car door
telling me stories
about your dad in Sacramento
How he'd buy you Mars bars
cutting them into four parts

You sent me Hershey Kisses
blowing off chores
Geography homework
hiding cigarettes from your mom
so she'd stop smoking
so she could
say my name
without choking on the last syllable

Placing your orange toque on my head
a crown of warmth
in the middle of winter

No Point in Asking

You said you're in
cahoots with me
Fiddle with my black collar
hold my hand
tan skin in tan skin

We stare at the clock
Half past seven
After twenty minutes
"cahoots?"
who says cahoots?
Fathers from the fifties
and people who call you
to make sure you're getting home safe
They pick at your hat
tan jacket
watch everything you eat
Stroke your hips slowly
so they can remember the parts of you
you hide so often

You must think I'm daft

Your tan hand
grasps my tan hand
Watch the clock

Half past eight
Can the seconds
last longer
than seconds
than minutes
hours

Another twenty minutes pass
You haven't answered
Instead, distract me
with half assed jokes
attempt to make me laugh
Nuzzle my neck
another natural touch

I'll See You Friday

Last bus of the night
We are waiting
to say goodbye
You are waiting
to let me go
until Friday

I can't see your face
when you hold me
but I can feel your chest
against my ear
hear your heart beat
faster
always faster
(you were never used to me)
Louder than
the thoughts I have at night
while passing street lamps
the headaches that are
traffic lights

When I won't see you
tomorrow
I think of the indent
on your upper back
how it curves toward your neck

The wetness of your eyes
while we lay in bed
whispering about the last bus time
A faint smell of fruit punch
your shirts always have
from the deodorant you got on sale
when we wandered empty malls
every Thursday morning

You wait for the bus to pass
its headlights that glare
white light
a wave over your shoulders
The shade almost makes them disappear

And I watch for you
when I pass
watch you mouth
"goodbye"
from the street
So I whisper
"until Friday"
through dirty windows
of the downtown bus

The Yard

"I want to be alone."
The words vomited out of me
with uncertainty
And so your calls
letters
the occasional text message
went unnoticed
Instead
I used my feet

I walked along waters
stared at hulking grey rocks
their heads afloat
trying to breathe through
frozen waves
I took the bus there in high school
left a trail of shame
not making track and field
Bodies of able bodied girls
smirking through my sweat
Water I did not want to drink
a slap on the face
I told myself to keep walking

I walked by my old house
The rancher that had the biggest yard I had ever seen
At ten I ran across
comfortable in my olive skin and
purple overalls
Rolling through buttercups
weeds I thought were beautiful
I saw the neighbour peeping
through our broken wood fence
and left that yard
So many years untouched
the grass has grown high

I Wish I Could Erase My Messages

You said you'd call me
while I stayed at home
Cross legged by the mirror
I mouthed
"call me"
           holding prayer beads

At nights you wouldn't be here
in a club I couldn't recognize
Glowing girls
a whiskey
a phone
I've tried to reach you
your voicemail
           bleeds

You'd call me
baby
babe
my girl
Other names
that never stood out
I was an
           ordinary thing

In the flashing factory
you'd sit in plush
neon chairs
dial my number
Ten digits is all you need
ten digits isn't much
to spread legs
If not me
you had
           other things

Our Roots

Lying in bed
I stroke your hair
It's growing long, and I can see
little curls
at the nape of your neck
You haven't bothered to cut it
even though you hate the black
slivers of moon
left on your bathroom floor

But when you stroke my hair—
an ocean of tangles
the curly mess that leaves you suffocating
in the early hours of morning
hair I haven't bothered to brush through
since last night
before we laid in bed
before the sheets turned sideways

—you can't stop whispering
how nice it feels
running your fingers through something
that isn't guaranteed
to run its course uninterrupted
You couldn't grasp
what it means to miss someone

you were convinced
you loved
until today

So you grab your brush from the nightstand
and grasp my hair

Natural Therapy

Every time
we'd walk through the forest
by the highway
(the one they tried to clear)
you'd tell me stories
of your father

Never knowing what to say
my hand would rest on your shoulder
and I'd look at the evergreens
each needle
in frosted shells
from the cold

You let out air
exhale
smoke from your body
damage escaping
corners you'd forgotten
corners I remember

Sitting on a log
from the only tree
they managed to cut
before the town riot
we ate our cucumber sandwiches

and I tried to tell you
I'd never say goodbye
Zipping up
your green jacket
wrapping you
in vows

I Didn't Save Any Money

It's raining
I line my mother's yellow primulas
along the fence and bench
The porch hasn't been cleaned in four months
I remember
reading books there in the summer
Poetry collections, a biography
Trying to write something of my own

We sit together
cross legged, facing each other
I haven't seen you in a week
You have grown
inches
of hair
Wheatgrass texture on your face
You hold my cold hands
massage the palms with your thumbs

"We
      could
           live
                together
                        in
                              a
                                    year."

Massage my palms
I try to write my own
Dig holes by the fence
place pots around the bench
I grow along edges

What I Am to You Through Others

Your mother asked me if you were okay
the other day at lunch. I took it in
and didn't know what words I should have said
I sat translucent; I have water skin

I see the lamp disguised as your dad, a
shadow on my bedroom wall. He sees your
desire to move downtown. Overshadows the
doubts, he's blind from all the mistakes you wore

Maybe you're ready to see me tonight
underneath rusted street lamps, spotlight blue
A large shadow hangs, one you carry light
So I drain to sewage holes, passing through

They'll ask about me one day in the dark
You won't reply because I left no mark

Friends Suicide Together

We ate out that night
drank milk out of styrofoam cups, split
turkey sandwiches with plastic knives

My grey sweater neighboured
your blue sneakers by the water
You dipped your feet
a rock hit the side of your foot
the current too strong

I could only watch you
stay above water
until you turned a corner
I could have joined you
downed mouthfuls of water
I wouldn't have had to talk
to police and family
and myself

I would have let them keep the blue sneakers
even my grey sweater
it wouldn't have mattered
I didn't turn the corner with you
we were supposed to be in this together

We're Suffocating

They see smoke rise
from the lumber mill
it shut down months ago

Nothing remains here

Sometimes they swear
thick grey fumes snake
through streets
past the high school, through the forest
that swallowed up Heather
past the houses on where parents
take a last smoke
lean out kitchen windows
beyond dark driveways
and dimly lit streets

They close frayed cotton robes
climb cracked wooden stairs
to bed
Tomorrow they will rise
descend familiar steps
sustain themselves
through the thick smoke
of this small place

Walk Among Myself

You sent me out to walk along a trail to hear you speak
A time of day when white roses wail to hear you speak

In another time, the sky would never open up its gold
Shine across the path, a lighted tail to hear you speak

To touch dry dirt, to press brown chalk against my palm
Water has not seeped through. So frail to hear you speak

On my forehead is a sheet of sweat. It's clear I'm worn
My body is bedrock. Through cracks I yearn to hear you speak

Lion flowers wilt into weak bridges
Sweet bouquet I could cross, although I'd fail to hear you speak

An ache I cannot taste, your whispers too faint
But joonam, bruise and bend. I prevail to hear you. Speak

Different Rooms

When I try to stroke her neck I leave it rotten
"You're too big," she says. She doesn't hold my hand even
      though we're familiar

I have walls, white and wide enough to feel like dust
I want to burn holes through them, but I can't stand the thought

You tell me, "I dreamed about a man my height." I can't go too deep
In parks I talk to pigeons: they tear up with me

They feed me bread. The mother gabs on
Grass is brown. Parched. I have yet to see it grow

"Hold me, keep me, need me," I say. I want to be older
You're shapelier than I remember. I'm too young

Have you forgotten? We played Lionel Richie records
Your sister called me "wild eyed." I've dimmed down, I swear

I write to you at my desk. The bedroom is dark
You decay in there. I am so close to finding your height

I Thought We Parted Ways

Inspired by Untitled *by Safwan Dahoul*

I've been staring at these walls
for hours
Decided to wear
a green dress
to celebrate—
it's been a week since I've seen you
You insist the dress is grey
the walls grey
my skin
grey

I live in a small room
six
by eight
I thought that once you left
I'd see doors
a large window with a sill
a mint plant
maybe
But I see no openings

Blue light blinds me in my sleep
I can't make out faces
People I used to know
merge and melt white
I can't make out faces

in my dreams
I can't see you
me

After Reading Cosmo Daily

THE SECRET REASON YOU CAN'T LOSE WEIGHT
At night you blubber
over how they were never there for you
eating cubed cheese you got at Walmart
half price
WEAR IT WITH CONFIDENCE!
"I'll never look back,
I'll just look younger."
THE MOMENT YOU LOOK OLD
There's still a glimmer of hope
You're a reminder of decay
to put it bluntly
DROP EVERYTHING,
find out which haircut to go for
with our easy quiz!
Hide the straightener burn you got
while trying to hide
that crimped mess
THROW THOSE FAT PANTS AWAY!
(again)
Low calorie desserts
in full bloom
while stepping on the scale
lick the icing off the spoon

It's Always Been Our Burden to Carry

My friend Teresa entertained
your conversation about what kind of beer
was better to drink after sex
because she didn't want to come off
aggressively uninterested
a threat to your ego
That's why I snatched her away
when you went to the washroom
to "relieve yourself from Alexander Keith's."
Why we ended up going home
to avoid you finding her
You always find us

Yesterday I spent half an hour
in the nearest Starbucks
because your stare at the bus stop
made the world around too quiet
too focused on my face
the cut of my t-shirt
the perfume my mother gave me
that smelt like vanilla and cherries

One time I yelled at you
to "stop looking at me"
on a crowded bus
I was heading home

You weren't familiar with my neighborhood
but decided to let me be your guide
following me to the street I lived on
I counted the lines on the sidewalks
slowed my breathing down to
two breaths per second
only to turn around
and you'd gone

I Searched These On Google
To Avoid Searching You

Why did you want this role?

Responsibilities of a mother
(we can't remember going to sleep)
Why are mothers always angry?
(It's up to you to show them why they're wrong)

How can we be happy when it comes with a price?
(Families are like quilts)
Why are quilts so expensive?
(We weigh it all in fiber)

If I ate myself would I be twice as big
or disappear completely?
(You make me want to disappear)

Care for me like I'm not made of stone
(Stop picking away at me)
At night do you stop digging?
Mothers look for healthy babies
healthy daughters
lost in the dirt

I can't remember my childhood
(Mother did not weep for me—
what does this mean?)
I can't remember Mother told me
affection is not rated from the heart

These Small Occurrences

I wear black. Blend my foundation carefully so that it will
not crease. Line my eyes just enough to show that I'm awake.
Put soft pink blush on my cheeks to show I'm in good health.
Wear thigh high black boots because it rains so much a
puddle forms on my patio.

   I can't sweep it off.

      Before I leave I smell the chai leaves my mother put
together in a silk tea bag. Place it in my purse. Catch the
145. The bus is muggy. Windows are fogged up. My hair
that I spend an hour straightening turns wavy. Frizzy. I
ran each strand over six times in high heat. I didn't use
protective spray. I avoid eye contact with a man sitting
across from me. Look at advertisements. Got debt on
your back? Call us. Want to talk to someone about
sex? Call us. Tired of shaving? Buy us. I'm considering
whether I'm tired of shaving my legs, arms. Waxing my
face. Plucking my eyebrows. Grooming my body so
much I cry from the pain weekly.

         Get off the eighth
         stop.

            Speed walk through the crowd and
            reach the convenience store. It's hard to
            stay awake. Fingers run through the lines
            of caffeinated cold drinks until I find
            one in my budget. I turn to head to the

cash register and run into the man on the
bus. "Can I buy that for you?" He looks
like the same men I see on the bus every
day. Except today he is off the bus. In my
convenience store. Wanting to buy my
drink. "What do you need that for? Did
you have a long night?" He has something
in his teeth. "I've never been with an exotic
woman." He has something in his teeth
and it's brown. I sidestep him and walk to
the cash register. He slams a five dollar bill
on the counter. "On me." He waits by the
door to make sure I won't avoid him after
he just paid for my drink. He looks me
up and down slowly. He takes his time.
He just paid for my drink, after all.

Today's To-Do List

- Book a doctor's appointment for next Friday
- Make chicken wraps for tomorrow's lunch
- Shave legs
- Wax arms
- Wax face
- Pluck eyebrows and cry when your arms get too tired, too angry about the required precision. About the patience
- Go to the bank
- Buy an oversized coat
- Buy three hats that cover your face. Make sure they cover your face because you don't want anyone to see this face
- Go to the gym
- Listen to the recitation of the Quran while lying in bed, trying to remember the day you turned nine. You went to the mosque. You bowed your head. You ate buttered pita bread afterwards and smiled with crumbs in your teeth. You looked at the high ceilings and breathed out so much air
- Eat buttered pita bread until your stomach is too full to sit down comfortably
- Call Mother

- Call Mother again because she never answers the first time

- Call your boss and tell him that you can't make it in tomorrow. Or the day after. Or maybe ever because you've finally come to terms with the fact that you can't work somewhere that had a coworker make an Islamaphobic joke behind your desk

- Brush your hair with a boar brush so that the frizz will go away and you will forget that you are wilder than they think

- Pay your water bill

- Pay your internet bill

- Pay your credit card bill and grimace that you bought three thirty dollar lipsticks. Three. Because you didn't think you looked good enough in just one

- Pick up the storage keys from your father. Try not to cry when you see his fingers shaking, trying to pick the right key, separate it from the others, hand it to you. Close your palm and rub the tops of your fingers. He will tell you to "not sweat the small stuff." He always says corny lines

- Take a shower so long your chest starts to sting from the hot water. You refuse to use lukewarm, to be lukewarm

She Could Have Been Hungry

She passed
when they had gone to get bagels
They thought she'd fallen asleep
so dinner seemed to be
an option

"Resuscitation
was attempted
repeatedly."
Repeatedly
his father asked how this could happen
in a matter of an hour
In an hour
her gold skin turned purple
waxy
cool

The grey doors opened
on their own
A dream
His eyes held back
waves
A pale pink blanket cradled her
atop a lumpy excuse for a bed
They could see the trees through her window
evergreen and pleasant

A cloud of antibacterial soap
and rotting flesh
stung his eyes
He could not recognize his mother
He saw a floating figure
a sick woman
among evergreen trees

Later, sitting outside the room
his father's eyes
poured buckets of water
He gripped his son's shoulder so tight
it pulsed
"It's funny how it all boils down to wanting some damn bagel!"
he said, drowning

Born in Surrey to Iranian refugees, Nina Mosall has been published frequently in the Kwantlen Polytechnic University's literary magazine, *Pulp*, and in the literary magazine, *Event*.